Freddie Fernortner

FEARLESS FIRST GRADER ©

Freddie · Darla · Chipper · Mr. Chewy

FREDDIE'S DOG WALKING SERVICE
BY JOHNATHAN RAND

An AudioCraft Publishing, Inc. book

This book is a work of fiction. Names, places, characters, and incidents are used fictitiously, or are products of the author's very active imagination.

Freddie Fernortner, Fearless First Grader
#4: Freddie's Dog Walking Service
ISBN 1-893699-82-X

Illustrations by Cartoon Studios, Battle Creek, Michigan

Visit www.freddiefernortner.com

Printed in USA

First Printing - June 2005

FREDDIE'S DOG WALKING SERVICE

1

Freddie Fernortner squinted in the sun. His friend, Darla, and his other friend, Chipper, stood next to him. They were his best friends in the whole world. Once, they had built a flying bicycle together. It really worked, too. Then, there was the time that they hunted for super-scary night thingys in Freddie's back yard.

The point is, they did a lot of things together . . . because that's what best friends do.

Mr. Chewy, Freddie's cat that chews bubble gum, was laying in the grass nearby. Mr. Chewy was also one of Freddie's best friends.

It was Saturday morning. Just yesterday, the three had been sitting in the very same spot, thinking of what they could do for fun over the weekend. Freddie suggested that they do something to make money. He had a great idea, but he wasn't going to tell Darla and Chipper until that very day.

"Okay," Chipper said to Freddie that Saturday morning. "What's your big idea?"

"Right here," Freddie replied, digging into his pocket. He pulled out a wad of papers. Each piece of paper was small, about the size of a candy wrapper.

He handed one to Darla, and one to Chipper.

Chipper looked at the paper and the handwriting on it. Then, he began reading out loud.

"Freddie's Dog Walking Service," he said.

Darla read the next line. "No pooch too big, no pup too small."

"A dog walking service?" Chipper asked.

"That's right," Freddie said with a wide grin. "Remember that lady we saw yesterday?"

Darla and Chipper nodded. They had watched a lady struggling to walk her big, strong dog.

"Well," Freddie continued, "she said that sometimes she needs help walking her dog. I'll bet there are a lot of people that need that sort of help."

"But how are we going to make money doing that?" Darla asked.

"Simple," Freddie said. "We'll go around the block, knock on doors, and ask people if they need someone to walk their dog. We charge twenty-five cents for each dog."

"But your paper says *Freddie's* Dog

Walking Service," Chipper said. "What are Darla and I going to do?"

"You'll be my helpers," Freddie said proudly, "and we'll split all of the money evenly, so we all make the same amount."

"That sounds fair," Darla said.

"Sounds easy," Chipper said. "And besides . . . I like dogs. It'll be a lot of fun."

Chipper was right: they were going to have a lot of fun. Gobs of fun, in fact.

Little did they know that Freddie's Dog Walking Service was about to turn the neighborhood upside down.

2

"Okay," Freddie said. "First things first. We have to go and find someone who needs his dog walked."

"Where are we going to find one?" Darla asked.

"We'll go around the block and knock on doors," Freddie replied. "We'll just ask people if they need their dog walked."

"But what will Mr. Chewy do?" Darla asked. "I don't think he's going to want to be around when we're walking dogs."

Mr. Chewy blew a bubble. Then it popped, and he began chewing again.

"I think we'll have to put him inside for a while," Freddie said. He stood up and opened the screen door. "Come on, Mr. Chewy."

The cat leapt up and ran inside.

"Be good," Freddie called to the cat. "We'll see you after work."

The three first graders set out. They walked down the street, and up to a house. Freddie knocked, and a woman came to the door.

"Hello, Ma'am," Freddie said. "I'm Freddie Fernortner, and these are my friends, Darla and Chipper."

The woman smiled. "It's nice to meet you," she said. "Can I help you?"

"Well, we were wondering if you have

a dog that needs to be walked." Freddie pulled a piece of paper from his pocket and handed it to her.

"Freddie's Dog Walking Service," the woman read. "No pooch too big, no pup too small."

"That's right," Chipper said.

"Just twenty-five cents per dog," Freddie said.

"Well, that's very kind of you to offer," the woman said, "but I don't have a dog."

"Oh," Freddie said.

"Bummer," Darla said.

They said good-bye to the woman, and kept going.

And going.

And going.

They knocked on every door on the block, and didn't get a single customer, until—

They came to the last house at the end of the street. Chipper knocked, and an old man answered. They introduced themselves, and handed the man one of Freddie's handwritten notes.

"You know," the old man said, "I hurt my foot a few days ago, and I haven't been able to walk my dog, Buddy, as much as he's used to. How much do you young folks charge?"

"Twenty-five cents," Freddie said, very matter-of-factly.

The man thought about it for a moment. "You know," he said, "that's a fair price. You're hired."

Freddie, Darla, and Chipper were thrilled.

"We are? Really?" Chipper asked.

"We'll do a good job, sir," Freddie

promised.

Just then, a medium-sized dog appeared next to the man, wagging his tail and sniffing the three first graders. The dog was a mix of several colors: white, brown, and black. "That's Buddy," the old man said. He reached out and pulled a leash from a hook on the wall. Then, he hooked it to the dog's collar and handed it to Freddie.

"We'll see you in a little while," Freddie said.

"Have fun," the old man said, and closed the door.

"Wow!" Darla exclaimed, as they walked off the porch and onto the sidewalk. "Our very first dog! This is so exciting!"

No sooner had Darla said those words than the dog stopped in his tracks.

He sniffed the air to the left.

He sniffed the air to the right.

He sniffed up.

He sniffed down.

Suddenly, the dog let out a loud howl . . . and took off running.

But that wasn't the worst part.

The worst part was that the leash wasn't hooked to the dog's collar like it should have been. In the next instant, the leash was no longer connected to the collar!

"Oh no!" Freddie cried.

Buddy had gotten loose!

3

Freddie, Chipper, and Darla broke into a run.

"We've got to catch him!" Freddie shouted as he ran. "We have to catch him before something happens to him!"

Up ahead, the dog was running as fast as he could. Then, he turned into a yard, and vanished on the other side of the house.

Freddie, Chipper, and Darla kept

running until they saw Buddy. The dog had stopped near a flower garden, sniffing the plants.

"Buddy!" Freddie called. "Stay, Buddy, stay!"

The dog looked at the three first graders, wagged his tail, then turned and ran off in the other direction.

Frustrated, the three kept going.

"We've got to catch him!" Darla huffed, as she ran. "That man is going to be really mad at us if we lose his dog!"

"We won't lose him," Freddie panted. "Just keep running!"

The dog vanished behind yet another house. Freddie, Chipper, and Darla cut through a yard . . . and were relieved to see Buddy standing near the side of a house, beneath a ladder.

The side of the house was half painted, and there was an open can of paint at the top of the ladder.

Buddy was right beneath it.

Freddie, Chipper, and Darla stopped dead in their tracks.

Buddy was sniffing the ground, unaware of the three children standing in the grass on the other side of the yard.

"Buddy!" Freddie called out. "Come here, Buddy! Come on, boy!"

Suddenly, the dog raised his head, turned, and looked at the three.

He wagged his tail.

"Come on, Buddy! Get a move on!" Darla called.

The dog got a move on, all right.

He bumped into the ladder, which tipped over the can of paint!

Freddie, Chipper, and Darla gasped.

Chipper covered his eyes with his hands.

Darla shrieked, and covered her mouth with her hands.

Freddie's jaw dropped.

The paint was going to spill all over the dog!

4

Darla closed her eyes.

Chipper gasped.

Freddie shouted "BUDDY!" as loud as he could.

And, by some stroke of very good luck, the paint missed the dog. It spilled all over the grass instead. Buddy didn't even know that anything was wrong. He ran happily up to the three, jumping up and down.

Freddie was quick to grab his collar and hook the leash to it.

"That's better," he said. "You're not getting away again, Mister."

"That was a close one," Chipper said. "That old man would've been really sad if we lost his dog."

"Come on," Freddie said. "I think Buddy has had his exercise. Let's take him back."

They walked back to the old man's house, and he was happy to see them. Buddy was panting and looked tired.

"Looks like you gave him a good walk," he said, digging into his pocket. He pulled out a quarter and handed it to Freddie. "Here you are," he said.

"Thanks, Mister," Freddie said.

"Yeah, thanks," Chipper said.

The old man closed the door.

"You know," Freddie said, as he stuffed the quarter into his pocket. "I have another idea. We might be able to make even more money if we split up."

"What do you mean?" Darla asked.

"I mean . . . it probably doesn't take all three of us to walk one dog. Let's each take a block . . . that way we can all be walking dogs at the same time. We might make more money that way."

"Oh, I get it," Chipper said.

So, that's what they did. They took off in different directions, each going to a different block.

Freddie wouldn't have any trouble.

Darla wouldn't have any trouble.

Chipper, however, was in for a *lot* of trouble.

He just didn't know it yet.

5

Freddie headed over to Oak Street.

Darla went to Maple Street.

Chipper walked over to Hoover Street, where he got a dog walking job at the first house he went to.

The dog's name was Abby. She was a big, brown retriever, and she was very friendly. Her owner, a nice lady wearing an apron, was happy to have Chipper walk her dog.

"I'm cooking treats for the church bake sale," she explained, "and I haven't had time to walk Abby."

"I'll do a good job," Chipper said. "I promise."

"Hope you can handle her," the woman added. "She likes to run fast."

"I'll hold the leash really tight," Chipper said.

Then, he turned and walked off the porch with the brown retriever on her leash.

"So, you like to go fast, huh, girl?" Chipper said, as he petted the dog's head. Abby barked happily.

Then, Chipper had an idea.

"Hey, you know what," he said out loud. "If you like to go fast, I think I know what we can do!"

Chipper led the dog back to his home on Fudgewhipple Street. In his garage, he found his skateboard. He held it up for the dog to see.

"How about it, Abby?" he said. "How about I ride on my skateboard, and you pull me? Won't that be fun?"

Again, the dog barked. Abby, it seemed, was a very smart dog.

Chipper hopped on his skateboard.

"Ready, girl?" he asked.

Once again, Abby barked happily.

This is going to be a blast! Chipper thought. *And I get paid twenty-five cents, too!*

"Go, girl!" Chipper ordered.

Abby bolted, and Chipper hung onto the leash. Soon, both dog and boy were flying along the sidewalk.

"Good girl!" Chipper shouted as the wind whipped his hair back. "It's working! It's working!"

Chipper was having a great time,

twisting and turning, as Abby pulled him with the leash.

"Weee!" Chipper shouted, as they went around a corner. "This is the most fun I've had all day!"

Everything was going perfectly—until Abby saw the rabbit.

It was sitting near a bush next to the sidewalk, and when they drew near, the small animal ran.

Abby didn't give it a second thought.

Instantly, she set out after the rabbit, running much faster now than she had only moments before.

"Hey! Abby!" Chipper shouted. "Slow down! Slow down!"

The dog ran through a yard, and, of course, Chipper followed behind on the skateboard, holding onto the leash for dear life.

"Abby! Stop! Stop!"

The rabbit turned onto Oak Street. Abby followed, running even faster to try to catch up with the fleeing bunny.

"Please, Abby!" Chipper begged, as he

held onto the leash while trying to keep his balance on the speeding skateboard.

But it was no use. Abby wasn't paying attention to him. All Chipper could do was hang on and hope.

6

While Chipper had been hanging on for his life as Abby pulled him down Fudgewhipple Street, Freddie was walking a dog on Oak Street. The dog was named Lily, and, like Abby, she was all brown.

Darla, however, hadn't had any luck. She hadn't found anyone who needed a dog walked, and she met up with Freddie and Lily on Oak Street.

"I couldn't find anyone who needed a

dog walked," she said sadly.

"That's okay," Freddie said. "Just keep looking. Now that—"

Freddie was interrupted by a bark, followed by a scream. He and Darla turned and saw a rabbit being chased by a brown dog. They were coming toward them very fast, followed by a kid on a skateboard.

"Oh, my!" Darla said, covering her mouth with her hands. "That's . . . That's—"

"—That's Chipper!" Freddie said. He and Darla jumped back, leaping out of the way.

"Aaaahhhhh!" Chipper screamed as he went flying by. "Aaaahhhhh! Help me! Aaaahhhhh!"

"We've got to do something, Freddie!" Darla shrieked.

Thinking quickly, Freddie ran to a tree in a nearby yard, bringing Lily with him. He tied the leash to the tree.

"Stay here, Lily!" he said quickly. "I'll be right back!"

"What are we going to do?" Darla gasped, as Chipper faded out of sight.

"Quick!" Freddie said. "Let's cut through the yard and go get our bikes! It's the only way we'll be able to catch him!"

Quick as a flash, Freddie and Darla sped across lawns until they reached Fudgewhipple Street. They each ran to their own garage, hopped on their bikes, and took off down the street.

"Where do you think they're headed?" Darla shouted, as the wind blew her hair back.

"I don't know," Freddie replied. "But we'd better catch up to them soon! Chipper is in a lot of trouble!"

They turned onto Oak Street and headed in the direction where they'd last seen Chipper.

Suddenly, Darla caught a glimpse of him.

"There he is!" she shouted. "Up there, by the park!"

Sure enough, Chipper was still on his skateboard, still being pulled very, very fast.

"We can catch him!" Freddie said. "Faster, Darla! Faster!"

Freddie and Darla pedaled as fast as their legs could go, and it wasn't long before they came up alongside Chipper.

"Chipper!" Freddie shouted. "Are you all right?"

"Make her stop!" Chipper cried. "Make the dog stop!"

"She's not going to stop until she

catches the rabbit or she gets tired!" Freddie said.

"If I fall off this thing, I'm a goner!" Chipper wailed. He was really frightened.

Suddenly, Freddie had an idea. Still pedaling hard, he brought the bike up right next to Chipper.

"Climb on!" he said.

"Are you crazy!" Chipper shrieked.

"It's the only thing you can do!" Freddie shrieked back. "Climb onto my bike!"

Chipper knew this was going to be difficult.

It might even be impossible.

And, for sure, it was *crazy*.

But, like Freddie said: he didn't have any other choice.

"Okay, Freddie," Chipper said. "Here I come!"

Would Chipper make it without falling?

They were about to find out.

7

Chipper raised one leg.

The skateboard bobbled and wobbled.

The rabbit darted, and the dog turned. Chipper lost his grip on the leash.

The skateboard suddenly spun . . . just as Chipper threw his leg over the back of Freddie's bike. He wrapped his arms around Freddie's waist and held on . . . just as the skateboard was jerked out from beneath him!

Darla screamed.

Chipper shrieked, but he held onto Freddie. It was a miracle, but somehow he pulled himself onto the back of Freddie's bike.

He was safe.

"Oh, man," Chipper gasped. "You saved my life, Freddie!"

They slowed down, finally coming to a stop near the entrance to the park. Darla parked her bike and walked up to Chipper, who had just gotten off Freddie's bike.

"Are you all right?" she asked.

"Yeah," Chipper said, "thanks to you guys. I thought I was going to go all the way across the country!"

"Why didn't you just let go of the leash?" Darla asked.

"I didn't want to lose the dog," Chipper replied. "I knew if I let go, I'd lose her for sure. I was going to try and hold onto the leash while I jumped on Freddie's bike, but it slipped out of my hands."

"We have to find her," Freddie said. "We have to find that dog that was pulling you."

"Her name is Abby," Chipper said. "She's really a nice dog. She just likes to chase rabbits and go fast."

"Well, we've got to find her," Freddie repeated.

"I think she went into the park," Darla said, pointing.

They took a few more moments to catch their breaths, then set out walking to find Abby. They walked through the whole park, but there was no sign of the brown dog.

"I have a really bad feeling about this," Chipper said. "I'm going to feel awful if we can't find that dog."

"And this is the second time this has happened to us today," Darla said. "Some dog walkers we are."

"She's got to be around here somewhere," Freddie said. "Let's just keep looking."

They circled around the park, looking in the woods, near the pond, and in the playground.

No brown dog.

Finally, they decided to head back to where they parked their bicycles.

And they were very, very sad.

Chipper hung his head. "This is all my fault," he sniffed. "I thought it would be fun to have the dog pull me on my skateboard. Now we lost her. I'm probably going to jail for ten years. Will you guys visit me?"

"You're not going to jail for losing a dog," Freddie said. "Besides . . . it was an accident. You didn't lose her on purpose."

"Yeah," Darla agreed, trying to make Chipper feel better. "It was an accident. We'll go with you and—"

"Look!" Freddie suddenly exclaimed. He stopped and pointed. "Is that the dog?"

Chipper squinted. In the distance, where Freddie and Darla had parked their bikes, was a medium-sized brown dog with a leash dangling from its collar.

"That's her!" Chipper cheered. "That's Abby! It's her! It's her! I can't believe we found her!"

But, there was someone else who had spotted the dog first.

The dog catcher.

And right now, he was approaching the dog.

The dog catcher was carrying a big net.

"No!" Chipper shouted.

But it was too late.

In the next instant, the dog catcher tossed the net.

Abby had been captured.

8

Freddie, Chipper, and Darla took off running and yelling at the same time.

"No!"

"Stop!"

"Wait!"

"You can't!"

"Stop!"

"Please!"

The dog catcher was holding the net that covered the dog. When he heard the

three first graders shouting, he turned and
saw them coming toward him.

"You can't take that dog!" Chipper
pleaded. "I was out walking her and she got
away from me!"

By now, they had reached the dog
catcher. Abby looked confused and sad in
the net, all by herself. She looked like she'd
lost her best friend.

"Sorry, kids, but rules are rules," he said. "No loose dogs allowed in the park."

"Please, Mr. Dog Catcher," Freddie said. "My name is Freddie Fernortner, and this is Chipper and Darla." He pulled out a piece of paper and handed it to the man. The man took it, and read it out loud.

"Freddie's Dog Walking Service," he said, "no pooch too big, no pup too small."

"That's right," Chipper said. "I was walking Abby—sort of—and she got away from me. Please don't take her to doggie jail. I've got to take her back to her owner."

The dog catcher shook his head. "I'm sorry," he said, "but, there are rules about having dogs in this park." He pointed to a sign. "Right there," he said. "Read the sign."

Freddie, Darla, and Chipper looked at the sign. They read it together, out loud.

"All dogs in the park must be on a leash," they said.

"That's the rule," the dog catcher said. "Sorry, but that's the way it is."

"Wait a minute," Freddie said. "The sign says that all dogs have to have a leash."

"That's right," the dog catcher said.

"Well, take a look," Freddie said. "The dog is wearing a leash."

They all looked at Abby underneath the net. Sure enough, she was still wearing a leash. Abby wagged her tail a little, but she still looked very sad.

"So she is," the dog catcher said.

"Well," Freddie said, "if she has a leash on, then we're not breaking any rules."

The dog catcher scratched his head. "I don't know if—"

"Yeah," Chipper said, growing bolder. "She has a leash on. She just got away from me. Please . . . if you let her go, it'll never happen again. I promise."

"Me, too," Freddie said.

"Yeah," Darla said. "I promise, too."

The dog catcher thought about it for a moment.

"Well, all right," he said. "But, just this time. Rules are made for a reason. We can't have dogs running around loose."

"Thank you!" Chipper exclaimed. "Thank you so much!"

The dog catcher pulled the net away and let Abby go. The dog walked right up to Chipper and licked his hand. Chipper knelt down and gave Abby a big hug.

"You kids have a nice day, and I hope your dog walking business does well," the dog catcher said.

"Thanks," the three first graders said. They watched as the dog catcher got back into his truck and drove off.

"That was close," Darla said. "We got back here in the nick of time."

"Let's get Abby back to her owner," Freddie said, "and get back to Oak Street. I had to tie Lily's leash to a tree. I hope she's okay."

Chipper picked up his skateboard, but he didn't ride it. Instead, he carried it under his arm and rode on the back of Freddie's bike. He held Abby's leash, and the dog ran alongside.

After they had returned Abby to her owner, they headed over to Oak Street. Darla rode her bike, and Chipper rode on the back of Freddie's bike.

"I hope Lily is okay," Freddie said again. "We've been gone almost twenty minutes."

"There she is, right there," Darla said.

They all looked to see Lily, seated in the grass, in a yard not far away.

But it was the man standing behind the dog that made the three realize that something was wrong.

When they drew closer, they could see that the man looked very angry. He was pointing at something—a small, dark lump in the grass—not far from the dog.

Freddie saw what it was.

Chipper saw it, too.

Darla saw it as well. "Eww, gross," was all she said.

Freddie stopped his bike by the curb, and he and Chipper leapt off. Darla stopped, and she, too, got off her bike.

The three kids stared at the small, dark pile in the grass.

They glanced at the angry look on the man's face.

Then they looked at Lily. Her eyes were wide, and the tip of her tail was wagging a teeny bit. She knew that something was wrong.

"*Guys,*" Freddie whispered, "*we are in a lot of trouble.*"

9

Lily wagged her tail as they came closer.

The man looked even angrier.

"Is this your dog?" he asked, as he pointed.

"Um, kind of," Freddie peeped.

The man pointed to the small dark pile in the grass. "Then this belongs to you, too," he growled.

"We'll clean it up, sir, I promise," Freddie said.

"I'm going to go inside," the man said, "and I'm coming out in five minutes. If that pile and that dog aren't gone in five minutes, somebody's going to be in trouble."

The man turned and walked into his house.

"Quick!" Freddie said. "Let's run to my house and get a shovel! Chipper, you go to your house and get a bag!"

"What should I do?" Darla asked.

"You stay here and make sure nothing happens to Lily," Freddie said.

Freddie and Chipper ran as fast as they could, across lawns and through long yards. Darla walked over and petted Lily's head, but the smell from the dark pile was so bad she had to hold her nose.

Soon, she saw Freddie and Chipper running toward her. Freddie was carrying a shovel, and Chipper had a small brown paper bag.

"Has the guy come out of the house yet?" Freddie panted. He was out of breath from running so fast.

"No," Darla said, shaking her head.

"Good," Freddie replied.

Carefully, Freddie scooped up the dark pile with the shovel. Chipper placed the bag on the grass, and Freddie dropped the smelly mess into it.

"There," Freddie said. "Pick up the bag, Chipper, and let's go throw it away."

"I'm not picking that thing up!" Chipper said. "It stinks!"

"Me neither," Darla said. She was still holding her nose.

"All right, I will," Freddie said. He handed the shovel to Chipper. "Darla, you untie Lily. She can walk with us while we get rid of the mess she made. Then, it'll be time to take her home."

The three first graders held their noses as they walked, cutting through back yards once again, until they finally reached Fudgewhipple Street. Freddie wrapped up the bag, and threw it in a garbage can in his garage.

"I'm glad that's over with," he said. "That was kind of gross."

The three walked together, back to Oak Street. They returned Lily to her owner, and the owner handed Freddie a quarter.

"That makes seventy-five cents so far!" he said proudly. "Twenty-five cents for each of us!"

"Cool!" Chipper said. "Let's keep working, and see how much more we can make!"

"All right," Freddie said, "but let's stay together this time, so we don't have any more problems."

They knocked on doors until they found another customer.

"Well, I'd love to have someone walk my dogs," the woman said. "But I have six of them. Can you walk all six dogs?"

"You bet!" Freddie said. "We're experts! We've been doing this all day!"

"That's wonderful," the woman said.

Within minutes, Freddie, Chipper, and Darla were each holding a leash. Six dogs pranced happily around.

"This'll be a cinch," Freddie said. "We'll make a dollar-fifty just for walking her six dogs!"

"And they're not very big dogs, either," Darla said. "This is going to be really easy!"

Do you think that it's going to be easy for Freddie, Chipper and Darla?

Neither do I.

And, in the next instant, the three first graders found out that, once again, they were in deep trouble.

10

Now remember: Freddie, Chipper, and Darla were walking six dogs. They were running all about, jumping and yapping.

And getting tangled up.

"Hey," Chipper said to Darla. "Keep your two dogs away from my two dogs."

"You keep your two away from my two," Darla replied.

"Both of you guys keep your dogs away from mine," Freddie said. "They're getting all tangled up."

Chipper's two dogs were wrapped around Darla's dogs. Darla's two dogs were tangled around Freddie's dogs. Freddie's two dogs were tangled around everything.

All too late, the three first graders realized they had a big problem: they were all tangled up together, tied in a knot. The dogs had wrapped themselves and their leashes around each other, and around Freddie, Chipper, and Darla.

"I'm stuck!" Darla said.

"I'm tied up!" said Chipper.

"I can't move!" Freddie said.

The dogs yapped and jumped, but they couldn't go anywhere.

"What are we going to do, Freddie?" Darla asked. "I'm so wrapped up, I can't move a muscle."

"There's got to be a way to get untangled," Freddie said. "Hang on. I'll try to get this leash over here and pull . . . this . . . leash—"

He struggled as he spoke, trying to get the leashes unwrapped from around them. The six dogs weren't helping much. The more Freddie worked, the more the dogs ran around.

Finally, he was able to untie one of the leashes. Darla was able to move her arm, and she worked to free herself. It took a few minutes, but the three finally succeeded in untangling themselves.

"There," Freddie said. "Now . . . let's finish our walk, only we'll stay away from each other, so we don't get tangled up again."

They took the dogs around the block, careful to remain a safe distance from one another. When they returned the dogs to their owner, she gave them a dollar bill and two quarters.

"Wow!" Chipper said. "A dollar fifty!"

"That means we've earned two dollars and twenty-five cents today!" Freddie said. "And we're not even done yet!"

They continued up the street, knocking on doors, looking for customers. Finally, at the end of Oak Street, they found another person who needed his dog walked. It was a small man with a big white dog named Salty.

"Salty's been a bad boy, I'm afraid," the man said. "He's been digging in the garden out back, so he's all dirty. But I'd love it if you could walk him."

Just then, Freddie had an idea.

"How about we give him a bath for you?" he asked the man. "We're experts at washing dogs."

Chipper and Darla looked at him.

"We haven't washed a dog all day!" Darla whispered in his ear.

"It's a dog," Freddie whispered back. *"It'll be just like washing your hair."*

"Gosh, guys," the man said. "That'll be great. How much do you charge?"

Freddie thought about it.

"Fifty cents," he said. "Plus twenty-five cents to walk him."

The man thought about this. "That's seventy-five cents," he said. Then, he looked at the three first graders standing on the porch. "Okay," he said. "It's a deal. I'll go get my dog. You can take him for a walk, and then use the hose in my back yard to wash him."

Salty was big . . . bigger than any dog they'd walked all day. Just like the man said, he was dirty from digging in the garden. His paws and tummy were covered with dark brown patches.

"We'll have him back soon," Freddie

said, as they took Salty away on a leash.

"Yeah," Chipper said. "He's going to look like a brand-new dog."

They walked Salty all around the block. He was a curious dog, taking time to sniff anything he could. Then, they returned to the man's house and went into the back yard.

"Now we wash him," Freddie said. "All we need is some shampoo."

"I can get some from my house," Darla said. She took off running, and returned a few minutes later with a bottle of shampoo. By the time she got back, Freddie and Chipper had already hosed off the dog. Salty was soaked . . . and so were Freddie and Chipper.

"Who's giving who a bath?" Darla asked as she approached. She was laughing at Freddie and Chipper. "You guys are all wet!"

"This isn't as easy as it looks," Chipper replied. "He keeps shaking and spraying water everywhere."

As soon as Chipper spoke, Salty shook again, soaking Darla.

"That's cold!" she shivered.

"Did you get the shampoo?" Freddie asked.

"Yep," Darla replied. She handed Freddie a plastic bottle. Freddie opened it up, and squeezed a big dab of shampoo into his hand.

"Here, Chipper," he said, handing the shampoo bottle to Chipper. "You wash that side of him, and I'll wash this side of him."

Freddie and Chipper worked really hard, scrubbing the wet, white dog.

But something was wrong.

"What's going on?" Freddie said, as he

took a step back.

"I don't know," Chipper said. "There's something funny about this shampoo."

They stopped washing, and watched Salty.

"He's not getting cleaner," she said.

"No, he's not," Freddie said. "In fact, he's . . . he's—"

"He's changing colors!" Chipper gasped. "He's turning black!"

Sure enough, Salty's white fur was turning black. The three first graders could only watch as Salty's white fur became darker and darker. Within seconds, he was all black.

Freddie, Chipper, and Darla were horrified.

"He doesn't even look like the same dog!" Freddie said. "He's all black!"

Suddenly, a look of shock came over Darla's face. She snapped up the shampoo bottle and looked at it carefully.

"Oh, no!" she cried. "Oh, no!"

"What is it?" Chipper asked.

"This isn't shampoo!" Darla shrieked. *"This is my mom's hair coloring!"*

Now, they had a huge problem. Salty, a white dog, was completely black!

All of a sudden, they heard a voice coming through the window of the house.

"How are things going out there?" the man called out.

"Uh . . . um . . . fine!" Freddie stammered.

"Great," the man replied from somewhere in the house. "I'll be out to check on you in a minute."

Oh, no!

11

Freddie, Chipper, and Darla gasped.

"Um, give us a few more minutes," Freddie said. "We, uh, we want to make sure Salty is really clean before you see him!"

"Okay," the man called back.

"Quick!" Freddie hissed. *"Darla! Run back to your house and get some real shampoo! And this time, make sure it's shampoo!"*

Darla took off running.

"What are we going to do?" Chipper asked.

"We're going to wait," Freddie replied. "We're going to wait for Darla, and hope that Salty's owner doesn't come outside and see that his white dog is now black."

While Darla was gone, the seconds ticked past like hours. Freddie and Chipper were afraid that, at any moment, the man would appear in the window to check on his dog.

Then, they'd *really* be in for it.

"What's taking her so long?" Chipper asked nervously. Actually, Darla hadn't been gone very long at all . . . it just seemed like it.

Soon, however, they saw her running toward them, carrying a small plastic bottle.

"I've got it!" she puffed, as she ran up to them. "It's really shampoo, too. I double-checked!"

Freddie quickly took the bottle and opened it, pouring the syrupy liquid onto Salty's black fur.

"Let's get to work!" he said, and he and Chipper began scrubbing and scrubbing. Every once in a while, Darla hosed down the dog with water. Freddie poured on more shampoo, and they kept washing. Soon, the black fur began to turn white again.

"How's it going out there?" the man called from inside the house.

"Almost ready!" Freddie shouted back. "Don't look yet . . . we want you to be surprised!"

They scrubbed and scrubbed. Soon, Salty was all white again. He shook, and water went everywhere.

Without warning, the man appeared at

the window.

"Well, now," he said. "Look at him! You young folks did a terrific job. I'll get some towels, and you can dry him off."

The man came outside through the back door. He handed Freddie, Chipper, and Darla each a towel.

"Just holler when he's ready," he said, and he went back into the house.

"Wow, were we ever lucky," Darla said. "I don't think he would have been very happy to see that his dog had changed color!"

It wasn't long before Salty was all dried off. His white fur shined, and he looked very happy.

"Okay!" Freddie called out. "All finished!"

The man came outside again. "Well, Salty," he said, patting the dog on the head.

"You're all clean again."

The man reached into his pocket and pulled out three quarters.

"And you guys," he said, dropping a quarter into each of their hands, "are good workers."

"Thank you," the three replied.

"Come on, Salty," the man said to the dog. "It's time for your afternoon snack."

Freddie, Chipper, and Darla watched the man and the dog disappear into the house.

"I'm cold," Darla said. "I'm wet, and I'm cold."

"Let's go home and get dried off," Freddie suggested. "Then, we'll meet at my house and split up our money."

It wasn't long before the three first graders were seated on Freddie's porch, each wearing fresh, dry clothing. Mr. Chewy had joined them, too. He was sitting next to Freddie, chewing gum and blowing bubbles.

Freddie counted the money they'd earned.

"We made three dollars today!" he said with a wide grin. "That's a dollar for each of us!"

He split up the money, giving a dollar to Darla and a dollar to Chipper.

"That was fun," Darla said.

"Yeah," said Chipper. "It was a lot of work, but it was fun."

"You know what else would be fun?" Darla asked.

"What?" Freddie replied.

"Well, I kind of had an idea," she said. "I thought it would be fun."

"What is it?" Chipper replied.

"You won't laugh?" Darla asked.

"No," Freddie said.

"You won't think it's silly?"

"Promise," Chipper said, holding up his hand.

"Okay," Darla said. "Here's what I

was thinking. See . . . my mom and dad just got a new refrigerator. It came in this really big cardboard box."

"So?" Chipper said.

"So, the box is really cool," she said. "It's big enough for all of us to fit in. Mom and Dad are just going to throw it away, but I thought it would be kind of fun to build a fort out of it."

Freddie was silent.

Chipper didn't say a word.

"Do you think that's silly?" Darla asked sheepishly.

Suddenly, Freddie jumped into the air. "Silly?!" he cried. "No way! That would be super-cool!"

"Yeah!" Chipper said. "That would be a blast! And it'll be really simple to do!"

The three first graders decided right then and there to build a fort with the giant box in Darla's garage.

After all, building a fort out of a big cardboard box would be very simple.

But, then again, when Freddie, Chipper, and Darla do something, you never know what's going to happen.

And, this time, their simple box fort was going to cause all sorts of problems . . .

NEXT:
FREDDIE FERNORTNER,
FEARLESS FIRST GRADER

BOOK FIVE:

THE BIG BOX FORT

TURN THE PAGE TO
READ THE FIRST TWO
CHAPTERS!

1

Have you ever wanted to build a really big fort? One that you and your friends could play in, all day?

Well, Freddie, Chipper, and Darla thought that it would be a lot of fun . . . and they decided to do it.

Darla's mother and father bought a new refrigerator, and it came in a big box. Darla's father was going to throw the big box away with the trash, but the three first graders had other plans.

First, Darla asked her dad if she could have the box. When her father said 'yes,' she was very excited. She ran across the street where Freddie, Chipper, and Mr. Chewy waited on Freddie's porch. Mr. Chewy was chewing on a wad of gum, blowing a bubble.

"My dad said yes!" Darla said excitedly.

"That's cool!" Chipper said. He spread his arms wide. "Let's build a super-giant fort!"

"Yeah!" Freddie agreed. "Big enough for all three of us!"

The three first graders, followed by Mr. Chewy, walked across the street to Darla's house. The big box was in the garage.

"Gee, it's bigger than we are,"

Chipper said. "How are we going to move it?"

"Well, it's bigger than we are, that's for sure," Freddie said, "but it's made out of cardboard. It shouldn't be too heavy."

Freddie was right. The box was big, but it wasn't very heavy. But, because of its size, they couldn't pick it up.

"Let's just drag it across the street and into my back yard," Freddie said.

They tipped the box over. Then, they each grabbed hold of it and pulled, dragging it out of the garage. All the while, Mr. Chewy watched and chewed his bubble gum.

After struggling for a few minutes, they were able to drag the big box across the street and into Freddie's back yard.

"We'll leave it on its side and make a door," Freddie said.

"What about the ends?" Chipper asked. They flopped open and closed.

"My dad has some really sticky tape in the garage," Freddie said. "We can tape the ends closed so that no light can get in."

"First, let's go inside," Darla said, "and see if the three of us can fit."

That seemed like a good idea, so Freddie, Chipper, and Darla scrambled inside, through the open ends. Mr. Chewy was quick to follow.

"There's just barely enough room for us," Chipper said. "It's too bad the box isn't bigger."

They climbed out of the box.

Just then, Freddie's mom opened up the back door.

"Freddie," she called, "lunchtime."

"Okay, Mom," Freddie called back. Then he turned to Darla and Chipper.

"Let's meet back here after lunch. Then, we'll get to work on our fort."

Chipper and Darla each went home.

After lunch, Freddie and Mr. Chewy. went into the garage and found his dad's tape. It was silver-colored and very sticky. He carried it into the back yard and waited for his friends.

Soon, Chipper showed up. He and Freddie and Mr. Chewy waited for Darla.

But she didn't show up.

They waited some more.

"Maybe she can't come over," Chipper said.

Just then, the front door of Darla's house opened and Darla appeared. She saw Freddie and Chipper, and she waved frantically.

"You guys!" she shouted. "You're not going to believe it!"

"What?" Freddie asked, but Darla was already on the move, running toward them. She stopped at the street, looked both ways, and then continued running. By the time she arrived in Freddie's back yard, she was out of breath.

"What's going on?" Chipper asked. "Why are you so excited?"

"Wait until I tell you," Darla gasped. "You're not going to believe it!"

2

"When I told my mom what we were doing," Darla explained, "she told me that our neighbor on the other side of our back yard has a bunch of boxes."

Freddie's eyes grew wide.

Chipper's eyes grew even wider.

"Really?" Freddie asked.

Darla nodded. "I went and looked. He has a whole bunch of big boxes! He said he was going to throw them away!"

"Throw them away?!?!" Chipper gasped.

"Not anymore," Darla said. "I asked him if we could have them for our fort, and he said yes!"

"That's so cool!" Freddie exclaimed. "Let's go get them right now!"

And so, Freddie, Chipper, Darla, and Mr. Chewy went across the street and into Darla's back yard. They went to her neighbor's yard. Sure enough, there was a bunch of very large boxes next to the house.

"Wow!" Chipper said. "We hit the jackpot!"

"We're going to be able to build a super-huge fort!" Freddie said.

"It'll be the biggest fort in the world!" Darla exclaimed.

It took them almost an hour, but the

three finally dragged all of the boxes to Freddie's back yard.

And they got to work.

They taped boxes together and cut doors on the inside, so each box was a different room.

And the fort got bigger.

And bigger.

And sometimes, when you work really hard, an idea might come to you without warning.

And that's what happened to Freddie Fernortner, Fearless First Grader.

It was a big idea.

A *good* idea.

In fact, his idea was so good, he dropped the tape he was working with.

"That's it!" he said, stepping back and looking at the fort.

"What?" Chipper said loudly, from

somewhere inside the fort.

"What, Freddie?" Darla asked, poking her head through a window cut out of the side of a box.

"I know how we can make our fort even bigger!" Freddie exclaimed.

Darla scrambled out of the fort, and Chipper followed. Mr. Chewy stood in the doorway, chewing bubble gum and blowing a bubble.

What do you think Freddie's good idea was?

Chipper and Darla were about to find out.

DON'T MISS
FREDDIE FERNORTNER,
FEARLESS FIRST GRADER

BOOK FIVE:
THE BIG BOX FORT!

About the author

Johnathan Rand is the author of the best-selling **'American Chillers'** and **'Michigan Chillers'** series, now with over 2,000,000 copies in print. Rand is also the author of the 'Adventure Club' series, including **'Ghost in the Graveyard' and 'Ghost in the Grand'**, two collections of thrilling, original short stories. When Mr. Rand and his wife are not traveling to schools and book signings, they live in a small town in northern lower Michigan with their three dogs, Abby, Salty, and Lily Munster. He still writes all of his books in the wee hours of the morning, and still submits all manuscripts by mail. He is currently working on several projects, including the all new **'Freddie Fernortner, Fearless First Grader'** series. His popular website features hundreds of photographs, stories, and art work. Visit:

www.americanchillers.com

Don't miss these exciting, action-packed books by Johnathan Rand:

Michigan Chillers (reading age 7-13)

#1: Mayhem on Mackinac Island
#2: Terror Stalks Traverse City
#3: Poltergeists of Petoskey
#4: Aliens Attack Alpena
#5: Gargoyles of Gaylord
#6: Strange Spirits of St. Ignace
#7: Kreepy Klowns of Kalamazoo
#8: Dinosaurs Destroy Detroit
#9: Sinister Spiders of Saginaw
#10: Mackinaw City Mummies

American Chillers: (reading age 7-13)

#1: The Michigan Mega-Monsters
#2: Ogres of Ohio
#3: Florida Fog Phantoms
#4: New York Ninjas
#5: Terrible Tractors of Texas
#6: Invisible Iguanas of Illinois
#7: Wisconsin Werewolves
#8: Minnesota Mall Mannequins
#9: Iron Insects Invade Indiana
#10: Missouri Madhouse
#11: Poisonous Pythons Paralyze Pennsylvania
#12: Dangerous Dolls of Delaware
#13: Virtual Vampires of Vermont
#14: Creepy Condors of California
#15: Nebraska Nightcrawlers
#16: Alien Androids Assault Arizona
#17: South Carolina Sea Creatures

Adventure Club series: (reading age 7-13)

#1: Ghost in the Graveyard
#2: Ghost in the Grand

www.americanchillers.com

AudioCraft Publishing, Inc.
PO Box 281
Topinabee Island, MI 49791

**WATCH FOR MORE
*FREDDIE FERNORTNER,
FEARLESS FIRST GRADER*
BOOKS, COMING SOON!**